Strip

ANGELA READMAN

SALT

CAMBRIDGE

PUBLISHED BY SALT PUBLISHING
14a High Street, Fulbourn, Cambridge CB21 5DH United Kingdom

First published 2007
This edition 2009

Printed and bound in the United Kingdom by Lightning Source UK Ltd

Typeset in Swift 9.5 / 13

ISBN 978 1 84471 303 5 hardback
ISBN 978 1 84471 530 5 paperback

Salt Publishing Ltd gratefully acknowledges
the financial assistance of Arts Council England

1 3 5 7 9 8 6 4 2

Strip

ANGELA READMAN won the New Writing North Promise Award, and a Waterstone's prize for her poems and short stories. Her poems were published in *Unholy Trinity* by Iron Press, and *Colours/Colors* by Diamond Twig. She has had work in magazines and anthologies, and has been translated into Finnish by Ek Zuban, *Hard core (Tapani Kinunen* 2006). She won the Biscuit Poetry Competition in 2004, which was followed by her first full collection *Sex with Elvis*. Her work has been described as paintings with words, sharp, savage, dry, edgy, witty and authentic.

'Genuine work from a genuine new voice—a voice which will be heard. Sharply observant, savage and wholly authentic' —JOOLZ DENBY

*With love, cowboy hats and gratitude
to Andy for everything x*

Contents

Acknowledgements

Some of the poems have appeared in the following magazines and publications: "Tom and Jerry Transaction," *Hard Core* (Ek Zuban 2005); "California Parking" *Staple* 2006; "Bodil and the Pigs," *Iota* 2007; "The Glass Bottomed Boat," *Ragged Raven* 2006; "One Thing," *Dreamcatcher* 2007.

The author acknowledges the financial support of a New Writing North Promise Award and the Cultural Sector Development Initiative.

I would like to thank Paul Batchelor for his expertise, Jo Colley for advice, Julie Watson for proofing, and Kate Fox for the loan of her extensive hardcore pornography collection. Much gratitude to Andy Willoughby, Bob Beagrie and Sean O'Brien's poetry school seminars.

Poppies

I could have slept in the poppies for a hundred years,
and would not have thanked the one who woke me.
I'd have taken off the ruby slip-ons, rubbed the blisters,
and made inside the red my home.
I wouldn't have missed you.
A man wearing someone else's face
may have visited, yet would have been you just the same.
Courage is just another abstract,
like friendship, and all the hearts you seek
grow on stubbled stalks, clot
their residue onto your sleeve.

I could have stayed, not been your girl in Kansas,
waited for the wooden house and rocking chair
to cyclone their way into pieces, reassemble
a helter-skelter house above my head.
I could have never learnt to bake apple pie,
or dance with a field hand,
or be told I was too old to climb a fence
and sleep by the foal in the barn.

I'd let the gas lamp in there flicker,
and travellers approach.
They'd come into my parlour,
and take off their shoes.
My inviting room with the stove on,
so tempting you'd never notice
there's nobody home.

Since only the two of us were inhaling,
you could have gone on to the envious city
in your snow-globe eyeball.
Your scarecrow gait leaking blood for ravens,
Tinman crying that I slept on,
until his eyes rust to half shut.

You should have gone on
to buy paper poppies,
place a wreath on a carved marble dog,

and left us.
Just me and the lion
curled together in dreams,
feeding flying monkeys
that breathe in the dust on our skin.

Bodil and the Pigs

I

Bodil arranges a toy farm
on a paddock of rug, light
spills on the wooden beams,
across the miniature barn in her hand.
Her father returns from sea
with the swing of the door
a little too hard.

He crosses the kitchen
as if it were a galleon.
Song on his breath
and an armful of poppies
laid beside her mother,
and the blessed Virgin
with her back to the sky.

*'I'd like to take you
on a slow boat to China'*
swayed into a tendril of hair
on Mother's neck, as he places the wind
into the shell of her ear.
Fists pound flour
into submission,
as she turns his kiss
to her expert cool cheek.

Pollen-stained weathered fingers,
and eyes that turn like the tide,
so little colour in him
with those flowers gone.
Empty hands hanging like hams.

II

With both hands she holds the glass,
watches the beer inside make waves.
She recalls the spray in Father's voice yesterday,
in his boast, 'It takes two beers to get me out of bed.'

In the kitchen mother beams
at her brother making the sun run,
devouring the smiley face
from a plateful of bacon and eggs.

No one looks up
as the girl tiptoes past
with Father's breakfast
into the hall, careful not to step
on the cracks in the boards.

In the white attic room
her fingers graze his aspen grip
as she hands the glass he lifts.
She watches the swell, each swallow
like a penny thrown into a well.
Only then does he say 'not a drop spilled.'
The foam curls on his lip.
He smiles. She laughs
as he says, 'Bodil, tell me your plans.'
Downstairs fills with the smell of boot polish,
unravels ribbons for church.

Tonight she watches him step out
from the pulpit behind his eyes, the movement
of a confessional curtain in his throat,
as he quietly says 'It takes two beers,
to get me out of bed, and six to find my rest.'

III

Between skirts the girl looks up
as her mother tries to pass an exhibit at the carnival:
Medical curiosity of our age.

The crowd pop like corn round this stall,
gasping, laughing, jostling
to glimpse the world's fattest woman,
unflinching as spectators throw sweets.

The girl is gently led away.
From the corner of her eye she catches
the woman daintily untwirl shiny wrappers,
and, with her pinky out, eat.

IV

Drooling trees
and sighing dusk
over the rusted tin bath.

The girl steps in, looks up,
hands closing over
that place between her legs
that must never be touched.

Remember
God is watching,
everywhere,
Mother says.

V

The day the boar died
she stood staring at the sun
caught in its eye,
the smile on its face.

VI

Her father talked too long to that woman again.
Pig ignorant . . . swine, her mother yelled.
Bodil pulls her hat low, admires her mittens
knitted for the first day of term.
Our Lady rattles as Mother slams the door.

Children in winter all-in-ones
trudge to school like prisoners on death row,
unexpected colours in the snow, a lupin
flashing purple through fence at the camps.

The child walks to where she is ushered,
turns to wave, sees her mother slap that woman's face.

All day she clutches the little stuffed pig
she knows used to be pink. One-eyed
shapeless thing that no longer resembles anything
from where it has been over hugged,
defaced by love.

VII

In her freshly ironed daisy dress,
she pauses to finger magnolia.

Her mother marches
against a spring breeze,
her hand just a stretch away.
'Bodil, stop dawdling.
The devil makes a jig for idle feet.'

Behind the locked gate
the sow lies on her side.
The litter squirm to find their place
at a matter-of-fact teat.
Trotter, snout, a tangle of skin
make smells she breathes in and out again.

Mother like clockwork, gets faster.
The girl trails behind, eggs shivering
against one another in her pail.

No matter how fast she tells her legs to go
the distance grows further every day.
Mother so far away, when the child
holds pinched fingers up to her eye
a tiny mother on the horizon fits between.

VIII

The last leaf clings
to the old tree,
holds its veins to the light.
Teetering,
his hand on her arm.

IX

Miss smiles, children laugh
as she gets words wrong to the farmyard song.

The children sing 'The pigs go oink.'
The girl stands up,
stamps, 'No. No.'
She gets on all fours, nose rutting the floor
as she grunts and snorts,
makes a sound like the skin of a girl
being unzipped to let a wolf in.

X

She listens for footsteps in the afternoon,
any minute now, his pace always
a foxtrot sweeping up to the stoop.

Tentative sun
peering through cloud.
The quivering grass

as the mousey-haired boy drops off the feed
and her breath moves the drape.

XI

It is a sin to talk to boys.

She licks the welt on her palm.
Under a curve of branch,
cherry blossom leans into the sky.

XII

The knots of her fingers,
look like whorls of the shed door.

On the old couch by the barn
the moon reclines.
She hears animals breathe,
through a crack in the wood.

The rain finds itself,
drips into a trough
with her face in.

XIII

Her sister's stomach rises each day,
doubled as dough on the hearth,
something to do with the baby coming in July.

She runs outside to the beat of hooves,
heavy clouds and a gate banging in the wind
as they lead a stud into the field.

The mare is ready; tethered to a fencepost,
it contemplates a proffered hand of apple
as the stud nudges grass behind.

The girl watches, crouched low,
arms binding her chest tight as a tourniquet.
Drizzle mists her skin, flickers
men and horses into one flip book.

Farmhands shake their heads
at the stud's lack of interest.
A gypsy mare is led in from the field.
The stud bucks, skin tight.
He rears up, veins rippling into rivers
to cover the good mare. A quiver of nostrils,
waft of tossed mane
stirs fringe across the girl's face.

The men cheer as the gypsy horse is led away.
Nostrils flare to let in the devil
as the stud fights sky, pounds.
'He's really killing her', a fat man laughs.
He turns to look right at the girl in the hay,
as if he hears the sound of her breathing,
she sees him, the look in his eye.

XIV

Trains groan to the platform,
leave with a gasp.

Winter strains through the laths.
The sun looks lonely
in all that blank sky.

Overnight, as if by accident,
everything turned white.

In the waiting room,
the man's hands
look as if they have taken a plane to the sea
and heaved a lead curl of it home.
He whistles the first bar of *Slow Boat to China*,
lets it trail to spray to ask the girl's age.
When she replies, he says
'Oh, then you must know everything.'

The man says he will name body parts.
She will point to those she doesn't know.

Trains come and go.
Steam on the skylight.
Outside smoulders, glows,
smoky as a smile from a stranger
or the chloroform in his coat.

XV

A rumour of leaves
skiffle along the path.
She washes her hands,
sniffs silent stones seeping
the secret of the coming rain.

Last of the light
rushes into the stairwell.
The banished dog
licks up a trickle of blood
on the girl's ankle
and their shadows become one.

XVI

Veins meander
like the pathways of flowers
pressed into each petal.

She strokes
the sows ear
that has made the sun blush.

---

*   Bodil Joensen ('The Boar Girl') later appeared in a series of films
collectively known in the UK as 'Animal Farm.'

Life of a Porn Star

Tom and Jerry Transaction

The day I started nursery
I wore Tom and Jerry underpants
with a bow like a birthday on the front.

I experienced first popularity
as boys queued and asked to read
the comic strip under my slip.
One offered half a Snickers
so I lifted my skirt.

It was the same day
I found a bird, dead on the doorstep.
Sat on the path with legs crossed,
the cold on my lap, blinking,
silently opening
and closing its wing.

Mom lifted me onto the counter,
gouged eyes from potatoes and asked
what I had learnt at school
and all I could say was 'something.'

Clear Blue Sky

A flap of sheets across my face.
A cotton skirt with my shadow across Mom's hips.
She tilts her head; I stretch,
flick flaking paint off my fingers,
as the porch swing creaks a rusty violin.

We hold the corners of sheets in our hands,
part and come together,
pull taut, raise arms
to make even folds, like girls
in white slips country dancing in the barn.

It's here I ask again how she met Dad,
just another stranger with a bill to change.
Mom's hair, looped in a bun, held in place
with a pencil like a question mark.
I squint to the sky with her smile slotted in.

Like that . . . it changes, something shifts.
One day I won't ask, after raised voices
over The Lone Ranger. Hi Ho Silver turned so loud
it makes the china quiver and the TV set hum.
A clear blue sky, so bright I can't look it in the face.

Mom wipes spilled milk in tight circles.
All week my sisters play with brightly coloured toys.
I sell cookies to the lady next door.
On Sundays the washing gets done.
The porch swing still creaks.

Mom and Dad sit on the same couch,
with mouths I can't quite put my finger on.

Postcard from Route 66

The old house is a used stamp,
edges perforated where I tore it from
the sidewalk where Mom turned Raggedy-Anne.
Her blood has cleaned itself away to the gutter
and taken itself all the way to the sea.

Dunes may shift but I'll comb the sands, as if I can find
broken chains, a small pearl, all of her that has been lost.
We will churn out of who we have been,
and onto Route 66 on a ticking bus
so silver it slices the sun.

Dinner With No Name

I

Dad serves cabbage rolls onto my plate.
His careful positioning of the greens
balances colours and leaves no two foods touching.
A steady river of gravy covers the cracks.

'When is Mom coming home?'

He chews my leftover rind. I watch
the twitch of his jaw, the slow up and down
of his closed mouth like a cave I crawl in to find answers,
as he butters more bread with one hand.

II

Dad can make almost anything.
We bake every Saturday, all night I eat
as if I can get enough of him to last me the week.
His Clint Eastwood eyes watch, narrow as slots.

He hands me the rolling pin. I roll
the dough that was flour just a moment before.
My featureless landscape he transfers to the dish
and with tucked lips shows me how to flute the edges.

My careful fingers follow his around the rim.
I press myself into a helper, a worker, my father's daughter,
branded, by flour on my cheek in the shape of a thumb.

Laundry Day

Dad's profile is a lace curtain I've memorized,
traced every vine and stem. His pruning sheers in holster,
hand on hose, a rock face under sky that hardly contains him.

On the clothes line wooden peg people fidget.
The dolly sister I felt-tipped with lips like an O
is speechless as the colours run.

Mom's face haunts the paddling pool in the yard,
turned into a jigsaw with pieces missing, rippling
as someone who looked like Dad shook vowels out of her.

Now it is so quiet you can hear feathers in the air;
the tiny fingers of birds separate and slap the sky.
I bring in the laundry and leave the people outside.

Last in the line-up,
Dad's peg with socks between his legs
and an expression stolen by the sun.

Me beside him, with a face I've yet to draw.

There Will Be No Time For Kisses

Dad honks twice, we clamber in.
My knuckles are white as lies
as they clutch the dash in the pick-up.
He whistles *Homeward Bound* and my sisters sing.
Mom watches us leave, but we do not look
at her eyes in the rear-view as we pull into the weekend.

She does not wave.
Her face at the window
reminds me of the woman next door
who always watched the school run.
A woman I almost saw the day after she died,
the stretch of her smile like a habit left behind,
faint as a thumbprint on the glass.

Blossom

When Dad's buddy helped lay the lawn
I was a cartwheel waiting to happen,
wanted to see how it was done.
I collected cherry blossoms,
felt their secret snow of spring in my hand.
The curtains twitched as I swayed
in and out the screen door.

The sun was an egg crackling.
The men ran hands through their hair,
patted sweat to leave their faces on their shirts.
I was permitted to take out the Bruskis.
There was the serious business of flattening,
but Dad's buddy was never too busy
to turn the sprinkler on me.

When he came with the mower,
he hoisted me up on his shoulders,
into the kitchen to help Grams.
I took a sticker off the groceries
to pop *New improved formula* on his nose.
I giggled, *Try me, you'll love me or your money back*
slapped on my dress as Dad walked in.

'Be careful, that's where she's starting to grow-up.
She's . . . you know, blossoming.'

Postcard from Hotel California

A picture of a greyhound on the side of a bus
I imagine will always make me smile.
The old man smells of pomade,
the daisies in his hand are lightning rod straight.
A woman leaves her good lips on an egg sandwich
and my sister hurls into a *Playboy*
someone tucked into the seat.

My head is full of *Hotel California*.
I picture myself with Malibu skin at a dresser,
combing my hair with fingers of sun.
My life will be palm trees,
a crowd scene on a beach. Somewhere
on the postcard is a pinpoint of colour,
you can't quite make out: she is me.

Tomatoes

Dad in his dusty boots,
sticks his finger into quivering buds;
the yellow on his fingertips
tickles each reluctant stamen.

Men pass on their way to the site,
but Dad does not see a thing.
He has crawled inside the mechanisms of flowers,
coaxes tomatoes to let themselves become.

Workers chat, whistle at the clack
of girls on their way to beauty school.
At the end of the day I slip under the fence
and collect empty bottles to trade for a quarter a go.

The house purrs in its sleep.
Crickets sing their invitations,
as I creep out to see our house from outside,
feel my feet slide in Dad's boots by the door.

It is as if no one lives here.
I make Dad's footsteps happen on damp grass
as I head to the plants,
feel the fruit in my hands.

One Thing

The leaves quiver an elderly hand,
so slight I need to adjust my eyes.
Rustle of breeze like a prom dress
being tucked into a car. I lie in long grass,
with the day on my face as my closed eyes bubble
with fields of rape, a tremble of yellow.
The hum of a tractor far away
as Mom's Hoover at the foot of the stairs.

I saw a picture of sunflowers once,
a fire of colour, so angry you knew it cared.
This is what it feels to be a cat,
just this, warm, light.
wheat licking my legs.
With my eyes half-shut
I have learnt to be my own Van Gogh.

Jake is here in slow swirls,
grass trails my nose
like his BMX circling my street.
The bread clips I saved for him,
to add colours to the brake lead of his bike.
My skin is no more than a reflection
of buttercup under a chin. So warm
the sun can't be bothered to wear his hat.
'*Hey sleepy head*,' a whisper like corn,
as he looks at me through the hair over his eyes.
He is so beautiful, a dream
I don't want to wake up from.

His light as bright as the fireflies
he caught in an old screw-topped jar.
As the sun slipped behind the roof tiles,
we gazed into their insect bodies,
heard the beat of wings like a shuffled deck of cards.

'See, we make our own candlelight.'
He has a beauty so golden I have to keep
its secret, before he is surrounded by fools.
My advice columns from women's magazines
Dad clips out and wants to label him with.
He has pushed me so high on the swings
a sound I never knew lived in me escaped.
And I was flying, really flying,
air beneath me, and feathers on my lips.

One thing, Dad said,
Boys only want one thing.

This face is a puzzle I think I've solved,
a something I almost saw
that made me love him more.
The day Jake's brother died I saw the sadness
and something they couldn't touch,
something maybe no one else noticed.
He squeezed my hand; I figured that one thing was me.
I made myself a ring of unshed tears,
diamonds I picked and polished from his eyes.

He is so beautiful the sky should weep.
I wait for the rain, feel only the glow on my face.
His cool hands make puddles in sun
that has emptied its bowl onto my skin.

Again, we play the wedding game,
the one day where we'll be happy ever after,
when we have followed the crumbs of each other
to find our real selves in a little wooden house.
His tongue draws the insides of roses
in my mouth, hair lisps on my cheek

as he says 'This time we'll play honeymoon.'
I don't ask the rules.

His hand in the darkness of a blouse,
no one has touched to find where a firework burns
and a heart thumps quick, quick as a rabbit tail,
a white you see in the woods, then is gone.
'Don't . . .'
'Come on . . .'
He stops for a while, and moves down,
fingers as deliberate as the outlines of all my hearts
drawn on a note book near his name.
'Please don't. I have to go home.'
I see the sparkler that has fizzled itself out,
fuming and grey as he wriggles away.

You play and you pay, Dad says.
There's two types of girls, Mom said about the babysitter,
She's not the type you take home to meet Mother.

I don't want to look at his beautiful face
that says I love you as he pushes his way,
takes the bad-girl that lives inside me
and pulls it out, back in, out again.

That sound coming from somewhere is me
unravelling like birds into Indian summer sky,
taking off in flocks and flipping a V as they flap away.
Is this it? Is this me?
Is this what they call making love?
That something that sounds so concrete
it is as if they have shaped it,
held it in place with words solid as nails
and afterwards put it into a box.

Maybe this is what grown-ups do.
Maybe everything will be ok.
Maybe he loves, he just loves me.
Maybe he will take me away.

The sun still on my face,
a crow-call someplace.
When this short forever is done
he kisses my hair, lets it fall
through his fingers like sand
and leaves my skirt round my waist.
His face is a zipped up fly
as he stands and turns.

I lie in the grass.
The sun slips to wherever it goes.
I remember the pink seal on Mother's cheek
when everything has gone quiet after.
I lie so long I leave my echo in the earth,
like the shapes of my parents in the mattress
I slip into when they have gone.
I stand in stages, arms and legs
a mime of something I can't name,
as I look. Look,
am looking to see that one thing.

The shapes of angels
our bodies have pressed
on the flattened grass.
A small heart shape
of blood on the ground
I'm leaving behind
as I walk away.

Stuff Dad Left Behind

1. The wax drawing on the fridge I did of family
   and had trouble staying inside the lines.
   Their cooling tower bodies
   buttoned from chin to heel. Faces
   scratchy as the table we pull out for company.
   No one asked why I replaced their feet with wheels.

2. A picture of his father
   with a meat cleaver in one hand,
   a goose in the other. In the corner
   a new tricycle.

3. The fancy chocolate box
   full of screws and nails.

4. An old coat,
   heavy with his smell.

5. A sculpture I made. His chest is an egg box,
   if you put them on walls you can't hear a thing.
   Six cavities in his chest, a paper doll glued in one.
   You can pull me out, and stuff me back in.
   A toilet roll leg fell off, I taped it back on.
   Mom asked 'Who is this?'
   I told her God.

6. A Ford key-ring of silenced keys
   Mom soaks in the sink.
   The build up of a hundred workdays
   leaves rainbows, that swirl before they drain away.

California Parking

Mom's new friend walks the path in green socks
and sandals that do not make a sound.
Opens the door for Mom,
when there is nothing in her hands.
He looks into her face and waits,
the day he says 'I've got a surprise.'

Some old book she holds in both hands,
runs them over and over the cover
and does not look inside. Just a dumb book,
but for a minute I think she's going to cry.
Each time he comes he drops off groceries.
The counter is full when he collects Mom.

She says, '*Thanks, this old thing*'
and twirls in a new dress, smooth as cream
being poured on peaches from a can.
He holds out his arm, and she brings out that smile
I saw once, covered in everything,
at the bottom of her purse.

I fill up on Hershey's kisses.
When the old dodge pulls in at ten on the dot
I look at my watch. The engine ticks over.
California Dreaming on the radio.
Her laughter evaporates churches
I see through leaf veins on winter's days.

His bald spot through steamed up car windows.
Her laughter on the breeze, and her hand
fiddling with the back of her hair
like a one-winged bird.
With my finger, I write in the dust on the table,
'I am angry, but I don't know why.'

Right Before the License Plate Game

We drive all the way to the lake
in a green camper van. My sisters
play Happy Families up front.

I dream I walk into an ocean at night,
opening its arms like a giant white swan.

The smell of thermos coffee wakes me.
A tickle like feathers uncurling from my chest.
Mom's friend standing near.
My tube top fallen down.

A look on his face that won't let me catch it
before he yells, 'Hey Sleeping Beauty's top fell down.'
He laughs, 'Look at her
covering her little poached eggs!'

Milk and Cigarettes

'This time it'll be different.
He really cares for us.
It's only temporary,
till we find a proper home.'

I nod, placing captions over Mom's head
before each sentence is out.
Even her voice isn't sure
whether it believes itself anymore.

The next day I think she's read my diary,
when she looks at me before work,
and with eyes sure as quicksand
says 'We should talk.'

My sister squirms on my lap
as I force her feet into socks.
'Don't forget the groceries.'
Her hand touches mine unnecessarily
as she hands over the shopping list and notes.

She looks at me
and does not see her daughter
has made herself as absent as the man
who went to the store for milk and cigarettes
and never came back, years ago.

Page from a Teenage Diary

Love becomes official by an initial on my chest;
his jacket tells people I really belong.
My name has an *and* after it,
sounds better that way, right as a hand
that finally knows what to do with itself,
enveloped in the back pocket of his jeans.

One year to the day,
he turns on the shower
so his folks can't hear
and pours me a mug of champagne.
Bubbles whisper like seething tongues
before we go all the way.

It's not so bad,
only hurts a bit,
anyway it doesn't last long.

He says he'll take me to the US gig.
Show me how to ride his boogie board.
Sunny days and kisses like surf.
There's not a thing to worry about.
We made a deal he'll always pull out.

Head for the Hills

The Latino kid's eyes are a No Entry sign.
I show him my passport to downtown,
ten bucks, if he will tell me where to sleep.

Under the freeway runaways get high.
The youngest tells me he's Tricky,
coz he turns more than anyone else.

We are snails finding shells
as my body curls to his
and his head finds my breast in sleep.
We dream, on a couch someone threw out.

Cigarette burns shine in the streetlight,
edges sharp as an eclipse.
His skin is homecoming, just for tonight.
Scars on his cheeks like snowflakes.

The Free Ride

The sun falls into a movie backdrop.
I rub my blistered feet with polished fingers,
for the first time in a long time, wish for rain.

A sign says *Welcome to Hollywood,*
someone has added a question mark.
I walk long after the walk of fame sleeps.
Walk, Don't Walk with heels in my hand.

When a cab pulls over, offers a free ride,
the driver's gold tooth is sun before the storm.
His face takes on the neon that surrounds him;
strip club pink, convenience store blue.

Just a block and I am walking again,
after he says he doesn't want nothing baby,
other than a golden shower.

Brace

In the bathroom
I wipe steam off the mirror
to assess the little girl smile
peeking out from *Penthouse* stung lips.
Just like that I can be old enough:
a smile to catch up with my hips.

I will make myself my own sweetheart.
I imagine tomorrow will be my prom,
as I take out the tweezers and twist.
I'll walk in to The Porcelain Dollhouse,
in a cute gingham top,
as girls in outfits unfurl,
to stretch into the imagination of a man.
It doesn't look that hard. Easy
as the Dorothy Barbie I undressed
soon as I got home, slipped into a bikini,
put in a bed with GI Joe laid on top.

Tomorrow I'll strut in.
And once my sight adjusts to the dim,
every eye will follow me for a dance.
All it takes is a mirror
and a pair of nail clippers
gripping the braces,
to release each tooth
from its metal cage. I take a spoon
and scrape off the cement.

Burlesque

Think of the pole as if it was a man, love it. Keep on his arm,
never leave him too long. Dancing you learn, even style. Pay atten-
tion. Who looks best? Who takes home what? It's the girls with a
look who do well night after night, say a cowgirl or a cheerleader
type. They pay attention to nail polish, toes, the lot, it's not that
they dance better, but what they sell is pure fantasy. Guys come
for enchantment; a stray detail can break the spell.

I read about a Russian once, fell in love with a woman who never
spoke to him. A showgirl with a way of making you think you were
seeing everything, by the slow peel of the palest pink glove. The
extension of her fan—revealing, concealing like an opening and
closing wing. Burlesque: you couldn't show the real thing, the
trick was to make them think. This man went backstage and the
dancer was gone, the trail of her skirt like the tail of a cat sliding
out the door, her hand on an arm. He went into her dressing room,
held her satin glove like an unheld hand. Slowly he unfolded her
fan over his chest, looking in her mirror as he took out a gun and
squeezed the trigger. That bullet passing through the feather that
touched her skin right into him, turning the satin into a flower,
bursting into bloom inside his chest. That'd be the last thing he
felt, the stir of one glove. That's how good you can be.

The dance is only part of it; some want to talk, flirt, go home
feeling good about themselves. I'm a good conversationalist, a
therapist in platforms and tan. Ask what they do, take an interest,
then charge for the chat. You can't learn that, how to see in a
minute their dreams that never took, and be the girl who stepped
right out of one. I've been a girl paying for law school, pilot
lessons, Mom's hospital bills, all in one night. Sometimes I'm just
a story you've heard a million times before, a girl with a baby at
home, paying the bills as she looks for Mr Right. Each one thinks
they might be him. It's harmless. They go home to the wife,
maybe for a few days he won't mind taking out the trash; she
gets flowers, I make rent. Everybody wins.

Strip

I let the strap slip, slow as sunset.
Remember, this is simple as skin.

Again, I see the sun deflect
behind the carcass.
My father's prized kill,
hung by hind legs in the yard,
shimmers in ripples of heat.
My mother so convinced I'll be afraid
of blood dripping into the tin bath.
Drips of petals, drips of starbursts
congeal still. So ugly, it is almost beautiful.
The deer's hooves dangle, shadows cast secrets.
My reflection, still there, in a milky river of eye.
A drunken fly staggers over flank, insect feet
seem to extract words from flesh
I want to touch to read the stories it tells.
Father strips the hide
with more care than the kisses
dropped on Mother's neck. I watch
the language of winter unfold from bones,
with eyes like eyes from a magazine under Father's mattress
as hide comes off like a glove,
reveals the storm under skin.

The girl on the stage takes a bow,
collects bouquets of used notes.
Stripped to the bone.
There is no more.

Postcard to the Photographer

I am your centrespread, unfolding
into woman, naked,
but wearing my own dress of days.

Beware, asphalt elbows that never tan,
bikini lines and uneven tones, parts
more felt-up than kissed by the sun.

Catch the curves, leave behind freckles
on my left shoulder, crumbled
from a golden baked day at Bridal Veil Falls,
where words blistered then peeled off my skin.

I curl, I bend, I turn in your light
as you unspool the lane of my back, walk down it
as if you can find the knee socks left by the lake,
the blackberry bruises on my tongue.

How a Girl Could Do That

Because the centrefold must spread into real girl
sooner or later, I know this isn't Kansas anymore.
My reflection in eyes spun my bleach straw into gold.
Forget pretty dresses, butterflies on washing lines,
I opened out into them till they no longer fit.
Like a frock Mom knocked up on the Singer,
I wear my own skin, pink enough to hide blushes in.

The first time I smelt me beneath the Montana,
was my scent on a man, a heartbeat to the click of my heels.
My map of lipstick on his chest showed me where I really live.
Sometimes, I think only when my body is pressed
can I feel the full length of my legs,
that no hands can touch me enough.
My flesh calls and they always come.
A body is relatively simple,
I keep my tongue tied making circles,
and when I open my mouth I do a job.

Sometimes a man is a room I walk into
and won't find myself in. I accept, kiss and lick
the faces of each dead and unmoving president.
I empty myself out, a vessel under waterfall,
because a vertical smile is still a smile.
I lie back and try to find the wonder
of each pearl I made in the necklace I'm given
again and again, like every day's my sweet sixteen.

Postcard to a Future Husband

I read somewhere
about skin, the comfort of facts.

In seven years no one will have touched me.
Every inch he has handled
will have shed itself,
drifted into my pillow, fallen silent
into secret snowflakes
that land on your tongue.

How to Make Love Not Like a Porn Star

Teach me to not make love like a porn star,
make me a bed that has nothing to prove. Let's laugh
at unscripted noises; let's not care what it looks like.
Make my body forget what it knows.
Let me breathe in and out to the fit of your hands.
Let me let myself not always be camera ready.
Show me a picture of me not 'doing a Marilyn Monroe.'
Let me see that your eyes are not apertures.
Let's sink to cliché, let your eyes be rock pools;
I hitch up my skirt and wade in, reach down to return
dirty finger-nailed, with a fistful of small shiny stones.
Teach me to close my eyes without making them.
Teach me to expect no result, zoom in for no reason
on the cleavage of your chin my pinkie fits in.
Let us not talk about the size of anything.
Teach me to listen, find a gasp in your hello,
how you make it sound like the first line in a tall tale.
Let your tongue be a silver river. Teach me to sail.
Let there be hair. Let's mention things that aren't hard.
Let my breasts look unlikely in your fisherman's hands,
the blister from toast like snow globes I find myself in.
Let us wake with limbs tangled as Chinese puzzles,
and garlic bread by the bed. Open your eyes, lashes like
footprints of snow-laden birds; let me pull off the sleep.

Postcard from a Porn Set

My hair falls to where it should go,
my tongue is a sculptor, like summer
on a scoop of ice-cream in my hands.

The scene unreels me on silver screen,
as a sound guy tucks into a meatball sub.

I look into the camera,
as if it can grasp every season
of the kiss falling from my lips.

Like that baby, now show me pink.
The rest is white noise.

The final reel, a sudden picture in my head
of a doll's house that got old wasps built their nest in.
The doll I loved, but left behind, lying
in long grass, her face peeling off in the rain.

What the Agent Said

How were we supposed to know?
She walked in here like butter wouldn't melt
on those double Ds, all handbag and a decent ID.
Exploitation? It was *her* who exploited me;
never saw a fifteen year old with more balls.
A real Lolita, you know the type,
dollar signs in her eyes, anything to be a star.
Now there's guys who fucked her in all innocence
I feel sorry for, treated like perverts,
never work again. No one asks how *they* feel.
Yeah, I've read the book, well, half.
So you made movies *and* national news?
Boo-fucking-hoo. She *loved* it, the attention,
the sex too. In between takes she'd swim naked,
get it on with Sunrise in front of the crew.
Course I know why she lied, she had to.
Shit like that won't get you on Oprah man.
Only in America dude, in Japan
a girl that age could be *married* by now.

The Porn Star Letters

Dear Traci,

I have to find out more about the green-eyed woman on my
boyfriend's wall. I asked who you were and he said Traci, as if the
name said all I needed to know. It's true, I was jealous, because
you were right there, and the only trace of me is a neat pile I
made of his magazines. All week you stalked me, every move I
made you were just two steps behind. I didn't know why. What do
you want? Standing there like that, with the wind beckoned for
your hair, ripped denim shirt, hand on hip, and your face like a
dare? I asked Billy what the picture means, and he said how the
hell should he know (I must learn to let these things go).

I can tell you are a people sort of person, but won't suffer fools
gladly, so I'm not sure where I fit in. Just yesterday I saw you, when
I forgot to look over my shoulder there you were to remind me of
something I'm not sure I want to know, striding pretty on a calen-
dar in my father's garage. It's nice how you bring people together,
seems you are the only thing my boyfriend and Dad agree on.

When they took the photo you weren't that much older than me.
But it's hard to believe, there's nothing in those eyes to say even
the memory of hula hoops and year books is still there. Not much
older, but I know if you'd been at my High School you'd be too
pretty and popular to be my BFF. You are looking forward,
straight on, just like when I leave home I'll never look back.

Anyway, I'm sure you have parties to go to (I am grounded, but
don't know why). You will probably never get this letter. Send me
a signed photo if you do. I want to learn to do my make-up like
you, and can give the picture to Dad for his birthday as a nice
little surprise.

Yours Hopefully,

Elizabeth

Dear Traci,

I've been checking the mailbox everyday, staring at your poster in Billy's room, but you are not here. His mom had brought cookies, says if he's gonna have girlfriends, better here than out on the street. Sometimes there is kissing, but I usually see it coming. A weird look on his face, when I can suddenly get up, stuff my mouth with chocolate cake, tell a joke, to cover the pounding of my heart. Sometimes it can't be avoided, I'll be looking at your poster and he'll land on my neck. This time his eyes followed mine, and he said 'You wanna see what old Traci does?'
I said, 'She's a model.'
'Nope. She makes movies.'
'She's an actress?' (that's when my voice went all Minnie Mouse, like I've been practising not to; what man will ever love that?)
Billy's face turned pleased as a cat, as he stretched his hands behind his head and said,
'I dunno about that, but she's definitely a star.'

Last Saturday his mom was out. His brother sat in his room firing Martians out of the sky. Billy closed the door in the lounge, and put a tape in the VCR. A bag of popcorn sat between us, but Billy didn't touch it (it's the first time I've seen him not stuff his face in the presence of food). I guess you were more important, something I can understand. I wanted to know how you moved, how you talked, didn't want to at the same time. At opposite ends of the sofa we watched you shed clothes and let a fat man touch you, his body as hairy as yours is sleek. Watched your nails grow and hand clutch a white sheet, knuckles paling and no sound but a gasp (I've been trying to remember your voice ever since, and that's all that will come).

It's not that I'd never taken Sex Ed (I saw a picture of a penis like a test tube) but I didn't expect all the mess. The way his thing looked as if it had been set on fire by his thoughts, burnt, angry, undulating into scar pink and shades of purple not on a colour chart. The noises you made, like pain and pleasure rolled into the same dough, mixing fleshy in your throat as the gorilla-backed man played the game of now you see it, now you don't. I busied my hands with the tassels on the cushion as Billy leaned back, and your golden crown bobbed up and down below the equator, like you were bobbing for hidden apples. Billy said something about your tonsils being removed, and I laughed like the tightening of a rusty vice. Your long legs, open mouth, something like pain at the teeth gnawing at my bubblegum heart, but I kept watching, the way I cricked my neck staring at road after a crash. You didn't seem to notice you were naked, wore your own skin as if it were a fur. You shut your eyes when you opened your legs (is mine supposed to look like that? It seems a little squishy and fat).

I was surprised how long it all lasts, how many moves were needed (you must have done well in gymnastics class). Billy grabbed my hand and put it on his pants, looked at me, as if he wanted me to see his knowledge of what you had done. Then I pretended I thought I heard his brother outside. Billy ejected the tape. The screen was dark; neither of us knew what to say. All I could see was our reflections. Me and him, with a body's space between, looking at our reflections looking back at him and me, on a sofa, in front of the TV.

Yours Sincerely,

Lizabeth

Dear Traci,

Again I enclose an SAE, for a photo of you it feels important to look at now and then. I don't know what you must think of me, last time I must have sounded so immature. I think I didn't know until I saw, didn't get how those animal moans could come from what they call making love. Couldn't understand how you could love a man with thinning hair and a Niagara of sweat raining in your eyes.

Billy has been teaching me what it is to accept a tongue. Maybe it comes natural to a beautiful girl like you, or maybe once you had to learn this too. The way he put it was funny, just like him, 'When you go to the dentist you let a stranger put his hands in your mouth—so what's so wrong with my tongue?'

Like a baby bird I opened my mouth and let him place it in, having faith this was good for me, and would nourish me some-how. After that come the hands, first over the bra I held on to as if it was virtue that would see me through to come out the same. Sooner or later the hands wriggled under. Usually I'm there to divert them on time, then one day you aren't. There is no going back. My body is like some drug he built up immunity to, because soon the top half was never enough. What he wanted is deeper than that, a finger burrowing like a worm, looking for light it can't find.

It happens in stages. It was as if we were rehearsing. After the bits of my body came the lying on top of me in our clothes (you get used to the weight, learn to breathe from a different place). More of the same in our underwear, and the prodding as it is moved to the side. There was no contortionism like the movie, and I remembered the sounds you had taught me that might make him pleased, but it was over before they found the right place. Maybe a woman like you takes more loving, and an ugly man must take more time to get you right, the way Dad never rushes a Cuban cigar, but can smoke a Lucky Strike on a two minute break.

[50]

Sometimes I think Billy is too cute for me, but the way he looks at me can make me forget I'm nothing to look at. When I am naked he puts me in his league, his hand running over my thigh and a wonder on his face like he has struck gold. That's the best, when seeing him see me lets me unsee all the ugly that I've seen.

I am getting better (I've heard people say some are bad in bed, and if this is something I have to do for the next thirty years I don't want an F grade. I've been practising to get an A). Billy said he doesn't know if you are an actress, but I think you are (either that or I've been doing it wrong). I have been quiet as an empty house, and this seems to make him ask how it was. I have started to pretend I'm you, pretending to be the dog when you rub his tummy, or the cat stretched in front of the fire. I close my eyes, imagine being half asleep, touch the strange bits as if they are slices of summer and I am making daisy chains under a warm sky, petal by petal of he loves me, he loves me not.

Yours as always

Beth x

Dear Traci,

I finally figured out the secret of your eyes; I bought green contacts
and they work just fine. It was after Billy and I split, the day I heard
his mates whispering and calling me a whore. I never knew there
was no point in sex for guys unless they can have you printed on a
T-shirt, to show the score of a game they think only they can win. I
guess that's something you know. But like I said, mine is a
bubblegum heart, not broken, just cracked and popped, chewed
into a different shape. It sits in me, waiting for pieces to be added
to make it taste new again.

OK, so I'm never gonna be Miss America, but it isn't so hard to get
a date with the captain of the football team, a guy so golden, just
to speak to him will make you a star. The first trick is to bleach
your hair, even an ordinary face can perfect a look that makes
him think 'I'm shy, but that can change for the right guy.' Then
learn to show a little knee.

When I finish school I want to do what you do. I don't suppose it's
that different, being expected to kiss after he has bought you
dinner, and being paid to do it for a film. I want people to look at
me in a way that makes me feel alive.

I wish you'd wrote a letter, but I know life gets busy for a girl like
you. I got a glossy photo, maybe you or an assistant signed, I put
in a frame by the bed (next to the one my parents got me of Miss
Memphis when I was a child.) Your writing was secretive, like a
spider with ink on its legs trying to die. I could just make out
your first name, and an inscription saying *Follow your Dreams*.

Lots of Love

Lizzi Beth xxx

The Bettie Pages

Momma and the Angels

Momma keeps a banshee in the closet,
blue vowelled and lipless,
the one she heard last night,
as Papa howled 'What's gotten into you?'
The girl knew. A blue moon
had slipped into Momma's skin,
wagged a bread knife as if were a tongue.

'Where's the woman I married?'
Papa rubbed his temples,
as if he could summon her from there.

All morning Momma sweeps cyclones
from raging dusty corners.
Her head is perched as a bird
on tendrils of neck in the kitchen,
a haze of unfolded hair,
smell of butter and Borax
as she leans over the table
and places a plate in front of the girl.

A pancake shaped like an angel
with deep-set currant eyes,
the girl fingers, and eats one at a time.

'Angel? How did it get there?'
Momma's eyes, as if someone just turned on the sky,
as she looks at the girl,
and stares into that plate
equally surprised.

The Glass Bottomed Boat

She rubs on the lotion,
takes the costume, makes herself a mermaid
one step at a time, as Father sets sail
in his old glass bottomed boat.

Tourists look down at manta ray
and take snaps of blue squares.
Another man with Hawaii on his chest poses,
arm round a carved wooden mast,
hand trailing a breast with paint worn thin.
She makes her face into a seafaring day,
wriggles both legs into one green latex tail.

The hours that boat dragged from her father.
One day she asked him why he called it she,
watched him sand the blisters, soap
the wood as if it were the neck of a swan.
Just like a woman, he said,
she takes money and work.

She brushes acrylic waves in her hair
as the anchor comes down.
The flotsam of all her questions,
dead seagull, old shoe, her mother, fish eggs
stirred to shale by rudder and hook.

The removal of her watch,
careful application of shells
before everything goes quiet
as she tucks herself in a coverlet of tides.
It was his idea not to get too close
as she swims under the boat,
make her hand reach for a second,
anemone slow.

He has told her a smile has to be taught.
She half turns, to be caught in a stare,
swims into magnified frame for a moment
raked of colour by the headlights of those teeth.

A dollar sign movement of a pearlescent tail.
No shape, but that of a mermaid
who always sings the same song,
collecting blown kisses that linger
in conches round her unfreckled neck.

She is no longer his daughter,
but a girl who has learnt the art of Mermaid,
who knows how to look up
at the blur looking down
with something like love.

Just a second, then she's gone,
guzzling air in the rowboat behind the rocks,
limp wig unfurling like arthritic hands.

Later, his words skim like pebbles
as he relates every gasp and counts tips,
tells the one about the businessman.
The guy who said he'd catch her,
marry her, go to the National Enquirer,
make a killing with her in his pool in The Mirage.

Her father makes towers of pennies
and she steps into that split second face
of his mermaid with eyes
that ask you to tell her of the sky.

Sweetheart

'Who is that girl?' I asked my pal.
'Don't waste your breath. The Duchess never goes on dates.'

That's what they called her, The Duchess, maybe because she was
like royalty in our ordinary Joe's dreams, or the way she walked
by, aware of her station, but not really seeing anything.
'She'll go out with me' I said, and walked up to her. She was
reading on a bench.
'Hey cutey, they got any more like you at home?'
(Cheesy, I know—but who could resist?)
'Yes, I have two sisters. Why don't you go bother them?'
She looked back to her book and turned the page.

That was The Duchess. We went out for a year, when she could
get away. One day I took her picture with her sister for her
momma, and when I asked how she liked it she made her voice
deep. 'Six kids I got, all wanting something all day long, what do I
need a photo to show me what they look like for? Bettie, pass me
the starch . . .' I'd run her home early, half a mile up the road and
watch her the rest of the way, merge with shadow as she ran
down the lane. Under the moonlight, the white of her bobby
socks like rabbit tails, her hair black as Lake Clare. The hourglass
figure I knew was still there as she turned the corner, the tilt of
her hips like falling sand.

In the service, I saw her picture on a GI's locker. A real forces
sweetheart, chest puffed out, and a hand on the nape of her neck.
'That's my girl' I said.
'Sure, mine too. She's sewing a button on my shirt, waiting for
me back home right now.' If I'd know I'd have taken more
pictures, more notice. In my wallet I had a snapshot of the old
gang and she's there. That's all I had, a photo that didn't look
much like her and a little poem she wrote me for Valentines—
but it wasn't the same.

Housewife

She will make herself pretty before you come home,
spray scent on her wrists, a reflex mist between her breasts.

You will walk into the kitchen.
Everything will be pristine.
The reflection of your hands on her chest
in stainless steel like a hall of mirrors.
You will swirl your keys on one finger.
Keys and fobs she notices multiply each year,
the way you clank them down next to her
as if their weight should tell her something.

She will get drunk on your breath,
mixed with the scent of Fairy that's kind to her hands.
You will kiss her as if she is a stranger.
She will wonder what you have seen
that makes you act this way today.

You will drink black coffee,
taken with a little sugar these days.
She wipes cupboard doors clean of the smears of fingers
and starts on the meal, tidies whoever she was away.

Irving Klaw

Mr Klaw men write in, I provide a valued service.
I'm a decent man, won't permit nudes.
A bit of leather, a gag, what's all the fuss?

The first time, the model turned the hobble
boots round and round, to inspect from every angle,
looking to find something she could understand.
Not a bad chassis, something about her face
like a slate you could draw anything on,
then wipe clean again. Who knew?

'If a dozen guys want a Thunderbird
there'll be one who adds a fancy radio,
one white tyres or red leather seats.'
My hands drew steering wheels in the air,
'Like a nice paint job on a convertible, see?
Different sort of client, that's all,
end of the day they all leave with a car.'

Cheesecake Snaps
The Faces of Bettie Page

BONDAGE BETTIE

Under devil horns she wears my favourite face,
serene, with just a touch round one lip
that gives away she is aware of the girl on her lap.
Her hairbrush mid-spank on the rump of a blonde,
like the one I watched over the fence
every night brush her hair till it shone.
That mist of gold like a halo
as she turned me down for prom.

BETTIE LOVES TO MAKE APPLE PIE

A wishbone of ribs, and concave stomach
where a teenage boy could rest his hand.
Her hair is a band on a black and white film,
as I read her lips and she bends over the cooker,
whispers what's for dinner,
lets me think I see my reflection
in her patent leather heels.

CLOWN DANCE

In a garter with daisies she sewed on herself
the queen of tease dances with a child's clown,
like one I had as a boy. I imagine a child, safely tucked
in sleep in the nursery, as time she comes out to play.
She serenades the stuffed toy with a parade of skin,
her eyes seem surprised to find the valleys and hills in,
as she looks into wide painted eyes
that seem to follow wherever she goes.

Jungle Bettie

Amazon woman
with a cougar on her lap
looks like she knows
how to build a fire, sail the raft,
keep her mouth shut.
Survive on the island
I sometimes wish I was on,
with a woman who'd let me rest
my head on a breast,
who'll take off her tights
and cast them out,
present me shyly
with a million small fish.

Cohabiting

All day I have been starving.
Frost on the path like babies breath
I touch, and feel cling to my gloves.
The gaze of neighbours at windows
pricks the back of my neck when I close the door.

In the hall, the cat is waiting to learn how to fly.
Yesterday I watched you place a sock on its head,
the moon-walk it made, your laughter I wish I'd created.

I scoop the flesh from a pumpkin, make a leer,
put the candle in, to surprise you when you come in.
I run my hands over my stomach to feel its dips.
I am aching to make you love me,
as simply as Bettie Page on your wall,
dressed as Mrs Santa, winking an in-joke
as she hangs a bauble on your tree.

The hours of your absence become preparation.
Time for me to alphabetise your books, ball socks,
get out the vacuum, nudge cream-cakes
smeared on breasts and the comedy cherries
in The Fat Girl Monthly under your diploma,
in the spare room, beneath the bed.

Heavy Petting Doris Day

I slurred every letter with an eager finger,
reading between the lines in Doris Day's biography.
I couldn't tell you why I wanted the words
to loop into whips and curl into chains,
at least spell a secret love beneath the bleachers,
when the sun hit the cheek of the girl next door.
The fine hairs there like peaches
she can see someone sink their teeth in.

Doris and a girl side by side,
keep a seashell of silence
in hands folded across their laps.
Hands that wait to be filled
with dog-eared prayer books,
pink plastic roses, small boxes
nestling engagement rings,
to peer into as if they were a mirror.

No music, but the girls waltz,
laugh like fine rain, uncertain
where to place their hands.
Doris looks down at both pairs of Mary Jane's,
slotted into one another like porcelain dolls
she had when she was younger.
China ladies she dusted with caution,
lest a curse peck its way out from such pretty shells.

Not so much as a trace of crotchless panties,
even a black bra, but I almost saw Doris
and the girl next door dancing till they got it right,
laughter making wind chimes of the breeze.

Girls dancing under the bleachers.
A kiss unfolding between them
like narcissi, blooming from lips
that say nothing as the sun looks away.

The Bettie Pages

I

I sat to paint the picture of my life.
I wrote out the title, my name
in the corner of a canvas, blank
with a sky white and waiting
for clouds to swirl into motion,
or the sun to filter through
to put tools into ready hands,
let words thaw or be frozen on tongues.

It should have begun with a woman
bending in a field with mud on her hands,
staking a pitch fork into the earth at the spot;
leftovers of the day spilling through the grass.
A baby wiped clean on a dirty apron.

The sun sank. Crows made pictograms
against the final fury of the day.
You can imagine her eyes,
how she held me up like a prize,
as the crows landed on the crop, drifted
one layer of sky at a time.

But Momma said only I was a quiet child,
and doesn't like to talk about that sort of thing.

If you listen hard enough,
in the dusk you can hear my first cry,
tolling along with the caw of a crow,
a sound that I must make to show I am here,
I will begin.

II

A mangle and soap, an iron, a hoe,
a log basket, a stove;
these are our tools,
the hands of family spliced from separate rooms.

Take what you can from the charcoal
of a small timber house holding vignettes
in one frame we sprayed for termites every year.

III

I could paint a child with black bangs,
so you'd know her, but my hair
grew uncropped till I was of age.

I could commit myself to a rose phase,
under a Tennessee sun, on the back of a bronco,
the girl you want blazing in oils.

A palette of colours, but I don't use them all.
The earth was a dust bowl.
Only know the fruit trees withered away.

A girl polishes buttons on Pop's uniform.
Breathing on brass, she rubs out pools of her fingers
and watches sun break into a dozen gold stars.

This isn't a picture that graces galleries,
but the one my hand lets me paint.

IV

What you want is for me to capture my father,
life size beside a mere thumbnail of a girl.

Even without a camera, something in my head clicked,
and the moment was frozen, imperfectly framed.

But how do I paint a whisper tender as rain,
as he says I'm his favourite girl?

Picture my doll face, its clash with Botticelli limbs,
if you will, the detail of stepping stone squares
of a wedding gown stitched into a patchwork quilt.
His hands—blurred and over exposed.

   V

In the playground, the orphan girls
make hula dances in a circle.
They sway like wild orchids in dust,
making puppets of the ocean with white hands,
as a little wooden house, all its yellow
and neat picture windows,
cruises by on the back of a truck.

The picture of my prom is one already sketched.
But the truth is I never went.

Through the locked shop door,
next to the counter, the brown bag
keeps the secret of a white organdie dress,
presses in its folds a pale pink corsage,
knuckles that might have grazed my chest.

VI

I step right out of a Hopper dawn,
to wait on a veranda soaked in stolen sunlight.

Two policeman, one with folded arms,
one squinting to make a view finder of his eyes.
'What did I tell you? That's *her.*'
I smile as they step inside, knowing
behind all uniforms are men
too shy to ask for autographs for Dad.

This Bettie stops in front of the mirror,
takes out two lipsticks and holds them out,
asks a flushing cop, 'Which?'
He points to the scarlet, looks down.

My steady hand follows the lane of a smile
with a gush of red. I buckle my shoes,
rub off a speck with the tissue
still blotted 'O' from my mouth stretched to fish.
My husband's children step forward,
at a nudge on their backs, to kiss me goodbye
with white as lamb lips.
Their father has become a basted man,
wringing the handkerchief
(he habitually mops his brow with)
as if it was my old heart or his,
as he says he'll be sure to stop by.

Jesus, as always, sends his love,
watches me drop breath mints in my purse,
call instructions to care for the bonsai,
how to keep the pond lilies afloat,

and I kiss his picture with my newly defined kiss.
'Don't go changing' I say.

In the back seat I point out good real estate.
At the Seven Eleven I buy Butterfingers
and say, 'The donuts are on me', with a wink
to the cop like a prom date on my arm.
On arrival, they say, 'Thanks for the Palm Drive advice,'
and, 'Watch your step on that broken glass ma'am.'
My toes poke into daylight, taut and bright crocuses,
as I extend my nylons from the car door.

The other me keeps a clean canvas.
A face that didn't want painting, caught
while the other Bettie was out to lunch.

A scrap of nightdress. A swirl of red.
Fingerpainted blue words
from the blood that found itself on her hands.

You don't need to see it take two officers
to pry the coat hanger from her fist,
extracting a Munch sky stroke by stroke
from The Scream raging under her skin.

VII

I sat to paint the picture of my life,
but it was not erased by any picture I can paint.

Bettie Page in a kitchen,
frolicking in surf,
straddling a fairground horse,
having the time of her life.

My likeness as prom queen,
cheeks pigmented with tea roses,
everyone in the scene is pastel mute.
A Doris Day negative, a teacher
in white gloves. I bring my own apple,
polish a Granny Smith on my breast.
A Bible school darling in teeth white pearls.
Aunt Bettie kneading a bake-sale of buns.
A middle aged woman clutching a license plate.

Or the moon bows behind the cloud
in my favourite photo never taken,
I am picture perfect as a nun
in my cell. I peer out the window,
the night makes a mirror,
hum 'Wooden Heart' as I brush my hair.

The real Bettie Page is a bikini girl,
she's a magnet on your fridge
to be placed under a series of outfits.

The work was fun, and I like the outdoors.
What more is there you need to know?

Lightning Source UK Ltd.
Milton Keynes UK
UKOW04f0832281217
314977UK00001B/85/P